The Future Is a Faint Song

The Future Is a Faint Song

Jaime Brunton
Russell Evatt

Dream Horse Press
Aptos, California

Dream Horse Press
Post Office Box 2080
Aptos, California 95001-2080

Copyright © 2014
All rights reserved

No part of this book may be reprinted without the express written permission of the publisher. For permissions, contact Dream Horse Press, Post Office Box 2080, Aptos, California, 95001-2080.
editor@dreamhorsepress.com

Printed in the United States of America
Published in 2014 by Dream Horse Press

ISBN 978-1-935716-27-3

Cover artwork:

Herds
by Rain Jordan,

rainjordanart.com

Contents

Epoch	8
Epoch	9
A Story of My Present	10
A Story of My Present	11
Poem of Miscommunication	12
Poem of Miscommunication	13
Leaving; An Apology	14
Leaving; An Apology	15
Mountains Mirror Mountains	16
Mountains Mirror Mountains	17
Tonal	18
Tonal	19
Fashion makes no sense	20
Fashion makes no sense	21
Mythology	22
Mythology	23
Epic	24
Epic	25
The End	26
The End	27

Epoch

The surface is as far as we need to see.
All that wants telling is told.
All that will be read is read. Singers sing
about first loves, dictators dream of suppressing
untold revolutions. All quiet for now. Where
on this earth have we not sung a song for our dead?
Where on this earth have we not lived and died?
The past is rich in suffering with stalwarts enduring
burdens yet unrecognized. We have just begun.
The future is a faint song. Something to break into.
The impassable side road leads to a beautiful ending.
Where have we not found the language of hieroglyphs?
The tongue of caves and belief in a gentler life?
Nothing pleases as much as belief. The sun
an easy enough emblem though made less
every bright morning. The hapless compile book
after book, read the future as if a collection
of straight lines. So many mysteries spreading out.

Epoch

For there is no other way.
For the higher calling is beyond our reach.
For the road we might have chosen was made impassable.
For everywhere, mystery.
For I have spent all the beautiful things.
For even the sky about seven.
For the cats care not for me except in their animal way enough.
For love is want of warmth given and a pleasing sound.
For nothing pleases as much.
For thou art the everlasting beginning.
For the hapless shall inherit some books from a friend.
For nowhere is it written.
For I shall need to watch my back while others need not.
For we care not for each other and are wary as cats.
For our wariness is not all of the same character.
For none shall make gentler this life.
For I will speak the language I have inherited.

A Story of My Present

I ordered *love on the rocks*,
got a hard look from the bar-
tender. "I'll take nothing off you
tonight," she said. It was
the first time I'd been there.
This made absolutely no difference.
Eight simple drinks later
at the all-night diner I was in search
of a problem. Found instead
a waitress with a shirt that read
Pregnant…and Loving It!
I watched the dirty business
of scraping the charred bits from
the counter grill. I sipped coffee,
tried to find some meaning in my
sham of a life. If I were younger
I'd be back to my old dumb ways,
drinking and eating alone. Now
I'm up to the new dumb ways.
It's a sliding scale.

A Story of My Present

Kids ordering beer in cans,
sidling up to the bar like old
stars. You get older and so
do I, measuring out coffee
in the dark morning, beholden
to the dark, its wonder
and deception. Where now
are the nights stretched
before me like a universe,
the cold light of stars piercing
my young heart? This,
too, must reproduce
itself elsewhere, leave me
alone in the kitchen
feeding myself, waiting
for the long day, for strangers
to reveal something
alive or about to be
between us—nothing
surprises me anymore
as much as that.

Poem of Miscommunication

Sometimes I wake up laughing at a joke I can't remember.
Or maybe there was no joke.
Maybe in the dream I couldn't read.
What else do you do then?
You cry or you laugh, forgetting yourself.
In real life, I never get as far as that.
I tried hanging Xmas lights inside the house.
We waited for the magic to happen.
It did not.
Maybe in the dream I had forgotten you.
Here, you would say, *take this.*
It's about to be yours.
And your hands would be empty.
Probably, I would not understand.
That would be just like me.
In truth, I was the one waiting.
Lights, as you know, will not induce transcendent states.
But this was a hypothesis I needed to test.
Maybe the joke had something to do with that.

Poem of Miscommunication

The saleslady repeats *make the sale, make it*
under her breath. It's already July
and I haven't accomplished
anything. I'm running in place, keeping
a surefire gait. She'll hold her own
hair, thank you. The joke where
no one laughs is still a joke,
according to one person.
I felt like dropping acid and stepping out
into the yard with the Xmas lights
and watching planes land
on the runway. The saleslady knows
it's important to remember the customer
needs to touch the item. *Here, take this,
it's about to be yours.*

Leaving; An Apology

All houses are eventually abandoned.
I can't afford to dwell on this. All we are

trying to do, he said, is affirm our existence.
One thing might do as well as another.

I've a gathering to attend wherein happiness
is the ultimate goal, and yet my studies

tell me we are setting ourselves up
for failure. So I pour myself into the arrangement

of playlists and soft lighting.
We all need an occupation.

This house will be abandoned,
though at the moment

we are dancing. How surprised we are
to find each other in motion.

Leaving; An Apology

For this reason, I couldn't afford
to stay at your gathering.

I put on my best forlorn
and limited your appeals. I took

one more finely poured bubbling
glass from the butler. I took

a spot near the wall by the limelight.
The house I live in

will be abandoned eventually.
Everything falls in the future.

Every evening
a big jumble of good times.

Mountains Mirror Mountains

In this land vines slip and weave into vines,
a slow construction for the hand
behind the pillar
of the self. The desert's sand
crawled in droves toward the sea
so the mountains could dare rise.
So thirsty was our god.
Now, each plant a minion of the sun,
a signature. The river a lonely pour
through the forest, an opportunity
for plants to baptize sickness
and let hope glisten on their leaves.

Mountains Mirror Mountains

Behind the pillar of the self,
mountains respond by changing
color with the season.
I am writing to you because
I want us to imagine mountains
in all forms of imagining: ascent, rock,
summit, and habitat. You see,
we are minions of the sun.
We want to recreate
ourselves eternally, in any form,
to give some part of us
a name, and let it go.

Tonal

I have been trained to respond to certain combinations of words well. Though this is different from what came before, even I have so many criticisms to sentence. Already I seem empty, like a word. These don't hear me, and neither I them. I find most of this arch and unpleasant. I cannot help you. The heart.

Tonal

I have been trained to hear certain combinations of tones well. As such I am delighted that this is not very different from what came before, even though there are still so many pages to fill. Already I am full like a page. I have been trained to be pleased in particular ways. What I please doesn't hear me. It deafens me to please. Tonally, I find most of this arch and unpleasant. What I am hearing doesn't please me. I need to hear familiar strains intermittently, that old feeling, they call it. Please help. I can't find the heart.

Fashion makes no sense

Finely contain yourself.

Fashion makes no sense. Noises make

a kind of self. Does it suit you something must.

Everything has utility.

Faced with sidewalks each direction.

Disturb what you can.

What makes sense to do so.

Fashion makes no sense. As a sentence might

a sentence may contain the noise. A kind

of sense is found in using noises well to fashion

give direction to a self. It has a utility

and so the same with each disturbance

in the sidewalks each direction. Fashion makes

no sense it suits you. Something must.

Fashion makes no sense

Nothing suits yourself like fashion.

Empty sense of cover.

Even the parking spots charge when empty.

Fashion makes no sense.

As a response might make

the noise it makes is.

My direction has the parking empty.

And so I suit myself. With sense.

With a something that must.

Mythology

Humorless ink stains spattered everywhere.

We have rendered the heart invisible

to keep the blood in as best we can.

We are supposed to love ourselves best of all.

I can't find the country it lives in.

We are supposed to know the others.

The map was drawn by a child.

Presence of mind not leading but led.

I imagine there are different levels.

Coolness like nothing but itself.

Mythology

Everywhere humorless stains.

I see the blood best I can, rendered.

I love no one best of all.

Others as well.

The map was drawn by a child.

I knew you'd find this mind here.

Before now, we jumped down

like nothing but ourselves.

Epic

For the epic is sung in all times.
For there is no space to admit otherwise.
No imagination leads us to the end.
Depth is an invention of limit.
For the evidence points to us in ways
we call small.
Revolutions occur quietly. The underground
is buried.
The narrative leads the way to already known heights.
For that endless present the future unwraps
domestic charms.
Rest is all we desire.
For rest is the essence of living.
For we have lived and died in all times and
we care not for each other.
For our wariness is not of the same character.
We are not the same character.
For this the epic is sung.

Epic

For the epic is sung in all times.
For where have we not lived and died.
For only the first loves are allowed in this song.
For there is no space to admit otherwise.
For the stalwart are as yet suffering under their burdens, unrecognized.
For we have just begun.
For a surface tells all that needs telling.
For depth is the invention of the unimaginative.
For the epic is sung in all times.
For the evidence points to all of us in ways we call small.
For the revolutions occur quietly.
For the underground has been buried.
For the narrative leads the way.
For to follow it is to ride an arc to heights and ends we already know.
For the past is as rich.
For the future is read like an endless present.
For we are looking for gifts and find none but the domestic.
For rest is all we desire.
For desire is the essence of living.
For we have lived and died in all times.
For this the epic is sung.

The End

At the end of this, a list to cross off as you go through the store busy with the purpose of flour, cinnamon, milk.
At the end of this, an amateur bathing in the fountain of relevance.
    A sad intelligence teeming with new rage.
    A garish ambulance venturing from the city in full flash and pomp.
At the end of this, me speaking in front of a classroom full of empty wooden desks, chalking up notes on the board for future tests.
At the end of this, a few bros tilting each other's trucker hats to the angle of *don't-blame-me-I-can-barely-read*.
At the end of this, is it really so bad to go gently into the night?
    Is it really so bad to bandy about terms of endearment, *Love you, Smack that ass, sure dear, as soon as we get back from the store?*
At the end of this, too much *this* and not enough *end*.
At the end of this, we'll all have a sip of what he's having.
At the end of this dingy stage, a sad measure.
    Dancing? Shit, dim the lights and slip into my arms.

The End

At the end of this, a puzzle, a river, a humid day, a spent fire.
At the end of this, a monster, a surprise, a trick, a reward.
At the end of this, loss, a reference to another text.
At the end of this, association, a sense of recognition.
At the end of this, your own face in the pool, in the window, on a poster tacked to a wall.
At the end of this, a punch line, a fist, a war, your cousin jumping out of a plane over the desert.
At the end of this, like everyone else, like your father, your mother, a stranger, a million
        people you will never think about.
At the end of this, credits, theme song, blank screen, lights, a pile of wrappers next to your seat.
At the end of this, flowers, a card, a hastily written note.
At the end of this, the unforeseeable, a thousand more nights, none.
At the end of this, a new road, a crash, an overgrown path, a thicket.
At the end of this, howling dogs, animal eyes in the trees, birds, always more birds.
At the end of this, regret, regretting, regrettable.
At the end of this, music, singing, song, a whistle, a clap, a metaphor.
At the end of this, image, imagining, projection, a stage for your favorite word.

About the Authors

Jaime Brunton's poems appear in *SPECS journal of art and culture*, *Denver Quarterly*, *Diagram*, *Cincinnati Review*, *Poet Lore*, and other journals. Originally from Shawnee, Ohio, Brunton currently lives with her wife and daughter in Lincoln, Nebraska, where she is an editorial assistant for *Prairie Schooner*.

Russell Evatt is the author of the chapbook *We Are Clay* (Epiphany Editions, 2012). His work has appeared in *Barrow Street*, *Cimarron Review*, *Lake Effect*, *Louisville Review*, and elsewhere. He lives and works in South Texas. Find him online at russell-evatt.com.

Other Winners of the Dream Horse Press National Chapbook Competition still available in print:

By Some Miracle, a Year Lousy with Meteors
        by Ariana-Sophia Kartsonis & Cynthia Arrieu-King
The World After Czeslaw Milosz
        by MRB Chelko
The Book of Evil
        by Jason Bredle